God Offers His

Kingdom

To All

God Offers His

Kingdom

To All

Volume 3

By

Farley Dunn

THIS IS A MYCHURCHNOTES.NET BOOK

PUBLISHED BY MYCHURCHNOTES.NET

COPYRIGHT © 2016 BY FARLEY DUNN

www.mychurchnotes.net

 THREE SKILLET

www.ThreeSkilletPublishing.com

God Offers His Kingdom to All/Farley Dunn – 1st ed.

Vol. 3

This is an original work created by
Farley Dunn for the website MyChurchNotes.net.

All rights reserved.

ISBN: 978-1-943189-21-2

Non-public domain scripture quotations are from The Holy Bible, English Standard Version® (ESV®), copyright © 2001 by Crossway, a publishing ministry of Good News Publishers. Used by permission. All rights reserved.

Dedication

Levi.

It's moving on that makes us stronger.

MyChurchNotes.net

Table of Contents

A Lawyer's Lawyer	15
Becoming Acquainted with Greatness	23
Buffet Bar Living	29
God's Gemstones	35
God's Generous Payout Plan	43
High Yield Accounts	49
Infringing God's Copyright	55
Magnetic Properties of God	61
One More Time, Mommy	67
Our Fine Feathered Friends	75
Stranger in a Strange Land	83
The Arms of the Snake	89
The Big Cheese	95
The Devil's Black Eye	101
The Man in Purple	107
The Twelfth Stone	113
Volcanic Christianity	119
Coming to Christ	125

Introduction

God infiltrates every part of who we are.

We do not have to know him for him to be all around us. When we take a drink of water, he is in the water. In the air we breathe, we find him there, too.

Imagine our children. They are us, and yet they think they are not. Yet, as parents, we never consider the gulf as great as they do. When our children hurt, we hurt. When they know success, we feel their joy. When they curse us and walk away, we want to see them come back to us once again.

Ask a child who is now grown. They will tell you they are what their parents have made them, whether good or bad. How is that possible? Because as parents, we infiltrate every part of who they are.

So it is with God. We can cry, "No! I am a self-made man. No supreme being formed me from the dust of the earth." And yet, we cannot escape our creator, for he infiltrates every part of who we are.

When we quit running and reach out to him, we will find him in every part of every day, and in everything we touch at any point in time.

He is there for us. He wants us to be there for him.

You will find God in this book. Look for him. He's waiting for you to find him, because he loves you very much.

Farley Dunn

Light Bulb Moment

There is no higher authority than God, and Jesus gives himself to us as our intermediary between heaven and earth.

A Lawyer's Lawyer

When we become entrapped in the legal system, the person who comes to our aid is a lawyer. This is a person specially trained to advise us on how to dance through all the legal footwork our judicial system demands.

Sometimes, though, just knowing the right steps is not enough. We need someone who will do more than advise us. We need someone to plead our case before the court; to encourage the judicial system to understand and be lenient; and to let us have one more chance.

We need an advocate.

In the United States, there is no practical difference between the terms lawyer and advocate, but there is a vast difference in connotation. A lawyer's job is cut and dried, giving advice as to how the current laws apply to our situation, and letting us make our decisions accordingly. Any advice he offers is based on the possible outcome of doing one action or another.

An advocate, however, does much more. An advocate assembles the facts of the case and tries to make sense of them, and then she presents our situation to the court to try to win us as much favor as possible. Our advocate may even help us dress to make the best possible impression on those who are hearing our case.

An advocate wants us to win.

Does an advocate have to be a lawyer? Not necessarily. Can a lawyer be an advocate? Absolutely. In court, we would expect our advocate to be well-versed in the law, and so we hire a lawyer to serve that purpose.

So, our advocate must be a lawyer's lawyer, both versed in the law and committed to presenting our case in the best possible light.

Jesus is our advocate before God the Father. He knows the laws handed down by the Almighty and how they apply to our sinful natures. He dresses us in our best, and he pleads our case before his Father to put us in our best possible light. He wants us to win.

Here are five of Jesus' advocate positions:

Advocate Position #1:

John 3:16. "For God so loved the world, that he gave his only Son, that whoever believes in him should not perish but have eternal life."

Jesus chose to come to us to learn our desperate situation so that he could plead our case with truthfulness and understanding.

Advocate Position #2:

1 John 2:1. "My little children, I am writing these things to you so that you may not sin. But if anyone does sin, we have an advocate with the Father, Jesus Christ the righteous."

Jesus recognized that we are not pure before God, and yet, he still stands before the Father, for he sees the good in us.

Advocate Position #3:

1 John 1:9. "If we confess our sins, he is faithful and just to forgive us our sins and to cleanse us from all unrighteousness."

Jesus is an advocate of second chances. He does not want the Law to cut us at the knees. Rather, he wishes to help us stand tall in him.

Advocate Position #4:

> Revelation 22:17. "The Spirit and the Bride say, 'Come.' And let the one who hears say, 'Come.' And let the one who is thirsty come; let the one who desires take the water of life without price."

> When Jesus pleads our case, there are no lawyer fees. He offers his counsel freely and without charge. He is the broken man's lawyer and advocate.

Advocate Position #5:

> Acts 1:8. "But you will receive power when the Holy Spirit has come upon you, and you will be my witnesses in Jerusalem and in all Judea and Samaria, and to the end of the earth."

> Jesus even promises to send us out with a dollar in hand and a bus ticket to wherever we need to go. He will never send us empty handed to perform what he requires of us.

A lawyer's lawyer is a person who is the best of the best. That's what a good advocate is, well-versed in the law and also out to make sure we get the best deal we can. Jesus is our advocate before the Father, and when he stands up for us, our lives will be made different.

In summary, there is no higher authority than God, and Jesus gives himself to us as our intermediary between heaven and earth.

Light Bulb Moment

If we want to become great, we need to seek out greatness in others.

Becoming Acquainted with Greatness

In 2014 an upcoming Christian film producer and his brother put out a movie that achieved acclaim in the entertainment industry. On his social media page, the producer mentioned having an opportunity to attend a dinner in Monaco and speak with the ruling elite of that chic country.

Then, as the 2014 World Cup soccer tournament kicked off in June of the same year, that producer posted a picture of him standing next to the legendary Brazilian soccer star Bebeto during the 1994 World Cup.

What is all this about? Even before his film company took off, this producer was becoming acquainted with greatness, and he continues to do so today.

Ten years before that 1994 picture with Bebeto was taken, this same film producer had another encounter with greatness. He attended a church summer camp in East Texas at eight years old, and he became acquainted with the greatest of them all: God. There is no greater goal than to reach toward the Creator of the universe.

> 2 Timothy 3:15 tells us that if we look to God's Word, he will open the doors of greatness for us.
>
> Genesis 1:12 lets us know that greatness will always arise out of greatness.
>
> Revelation 22:18 says that the Bible is the final authority on greatness.
>
> 1 John 1:9 assures us that we can find greatness in Christ.
>
> 2 Peter 3:8 looks to our future, for the greatness of Jesus is without end.

Too often we look at people around us, and we say, "Aren't they so lucky?" Yet we never consider that they were once eight years old, and they were once the skinny eighteen-year-old standing next to a prestigious star player, and they became great because they became acquainted with greatness.

Greatness doesn't just happen. Greatness is a

contagious disease, spread by contact, and promulgated by hard work and sweat. If we get next to Jesus, that's where it all begins.

In summary, if we want to become great, we need to seek out greatness in others.

Light Bulb Moment

When we visit God's diner, we will leave stuffed to the gills.

Buffet Bar Living

There are wide ranges of dining opportunities available to us. We can enjoy take out, drive through, or casual in-house dining, complete with waiters and menus. If we want to jazz it up, we can experience linen napkins complete with crystal and silver flatware.

Yet we get the most for our money at a buffet. Our choices are endless, with the meals laid out in an entreating display designed to tempt us to indulge.

We want to be at a buffet.

God's creation is a buffet of the most impressive sort. Let's see what God has provided on his buffet bar.

In the first display we find life.

Genesis 2:7 tells us:

> "Then the Lord God formed the man of dust from the ground and breathed into his nostrils the breath of life, and the man became a living creature."

> When we are born, we slip a serving of life onto our tray. We anticipate its aroma from the very first moment.

The second display gives us those things that share our world with us.

Genesis 1:24 tells us:

> "And God said, 'Let the earth bring forth living creatures according to their kinds—livestock and creeping things and beasts of the earth according to their kinds.' And it was so."

> This dish adds culinary variety to our lives. Its aromas mingle with those from that we've already received, and our existence is so much sweeter.

The third display is continued life.

1 Corinthians 15:51-55 tells us:

> "Behold! I tell you a mystery. We shall not all

sleep, but we shall all be changed, in a moment, in the twinkling of an eye, at the last trumpet. For the trumpet will sound, and the dead will be raised imperishable, and we shall be changed. For this perishable body must put on the imperishable, and this mortal body must put on immortality. When the perishable puts on the imperishable, and the mortal puts on immortality, then shall come to pass the saying that is written: 'Death is swallowed up in victory.' 'O death, where is your victory? O death, where is your sting?' "

This is our dessert, for once our first two dishes are consumed, we can dip into the sweetest of God's offerings, eternal life with the Father.

How do we receive this final culinary concoction? We find that recipe in 1 Corinthians 6:19-20:

"Or do you not know that your body is a temple of the Holy Spirit within you, whom you have from God? You are not your own, for you were bought with a price. So glorify God in your body."

When we live an upright life before God and the world, all of God's good things will be ours to consume, and that includes everything on God's heavenly buffet:

1. Our own life and that of all humanity

2. The creatures that share our world with us

3. Our eternal reward for walking with the Holy One

In summary, when we visit God's diner, we will leave stuffed to the gills.

Light Bulb Moment

When we become gemstones for Christ, we take on a luster the world cannot wear away.

God's Gemstones

A gem is a gem, right? The properties of each are simple to recognize. A diamond is clear, a ruby red, and a sapphire? Only the deepest of blues will convince us that our gemstone is a true sapphire.

The Bible speaks of many types of jewels, as if the various kinds make a difference. Maybe they do. Let's look at them and see.

In Revelation 21, we read of the description of the holy city of New Jerusalem. The walls are built of jasper, while the city is pure gold, so reflective it is like clear glass.

The next passage is where we want to pause, for the city's foundations are adorned with every kind of jewel: jasper, sapphire, agate, emerald, and more, twelve kinds in all. Let's look at the importance of these vastly disparate gemstones decorating the city's foundations.

Jasper:

> Jasper is high-grade quartz filled with impurities. It is these impurities that give the stone its ornate patterning.
>
> It is only when we are filled with God that we become beautiful to the world. His "impurities" are what make us perfect before him.

Sapphire:

> The rarest of sapphires have fine silk-like strands that can cause their reflections to change from light to dark with a shift of viewing angle.
>
> How like our God to be all things to all people! It is all in how we view him.

Agate:

> The fire agate is one of the most mesmerizing of stones. Its iridescence comes from different layers that cause light to separate into different colors.
>
> God is the same. He becomes beautiful to the sinner no matter how he is reflected through us.

Emerald:

There are two types of green emeralds, the true gem colored by chromium and the false stone colored by vanadium. The beauty of a true emerald is in direct relationship to its fragility. The two are intertwined.

Our relationship with God is the most beautiful part of our existence, and it is worth the care we must give it to preserve its magnificence.

Onyx:

We think of onyx as a black stone, but until it is dyed, its layers can be black and white, or even the more striking red and white. When carved correctly, one layer stands out in sharp contrast to the other, creating a vibrant effect.

When we present God to the world, he should stand out in sharp contrast to the carnal fabric of our human condition. The world will see him as beautiful.

Carnelian:

This reddish stone is one of the oldest known quartz gemstones, but it has distinct qualities that distinguish it from other types of quartz. It is translucent when held to the light, and it has superior hardness and durability.

It is Christ that gives us our carnelian qualities. Others will see him in us when we are held to the light, and we will remain strong when battered by the trials we must all face in this life.

Chrysolite:

Chrysolite is most likely the mineral olivine, known in gemology as peridot. It is composed of two minerals, and its name means "gold stone."

When we become one with our Father in heaven, we become something precious. We become a "gold stone" in the foundation of his kingdom.

Beryl:

Only a fraction of beryl is of transparent gem quality, and is known as "precious beryl." Many well-known types of gemstones are actually beryl, and can be identified by their distinctive crystal structure.

As children of God, we also carry distinctive qualities. Our religious affiliation is our color and cut. Our crystal structure is our belief in Jesus.

Topaz:

In its pure form, topaz is white. Yet, it can be distinguished from every other stone by its crystal structure and the fact that it glows with a distinct fluorescence.

The true Christian is topaz, for when we come to the cross, our spiritual structure is changed, and we will glow with the love of Christ.

Chrysoprase:

There are few stones rarer than chrysoprase. Actually a variety of quartz, its apple-green color comes from nickel impurities. Even under magnification, its crystals are too fine to be seen separately.

The unified body of Christ is like chrysoprase, rare, beautiful, and bonded too tightly to be told one from another. We become one in him.

Jacinth:

No longer used in gemology, the term jacinth is thought to refer to the reddish-orange zircon. It is one of the most important historical gemstones, dating to the breastplate of Aaron in the Old Testament. Zircon is the oldest mineral on earth with confirmed samples dated at 4.4 billion years old.

Finding God is like finding our jacinth. We have the original, the best, and the most important object of antiquity in our grasp. The great thing? God is as vital today as he was then.

Amethyst:

Iron and aluminum give the amethyst its brilliant purple color. The more iron we find in the mineral, the brighter purple it shines.

It is the same with us. The more of Jesus we let into our lives, the more brilliantly we shine for him.

That foundation of the New Jerusalem? The gemstones we find there represent the best that God has ever offered to mankind. When we stand in that city, we can be confident it will last for eternity. Its foundation stones tell us so.

In summary, when we become gemstones for Christ, we take on a luster the world cannot wear away.

Light Bulb Moment

The earthquake is unimportant. It's what we get out of it that makes us shine for Jesus.

God's Generous Payout Plan

We tease about couples who bicker with each other, saying, "She married him. She got what's coming to her."

Or, when our unfair boss is sacked, we say the same. "He got what he deserved." And oh, it feels so good to whisper those words to anyone who will listen.

Then, when the lottery is announced, we hold our tickets, and we groan, "When will I get what I deserve? I want to be on the lottery's payout plan!"

Do we really want what we deserve? It might not be the $50 million jackpot we hope for. Instead, God might mete out what we really have coming to us.

We might really get what we deserve.

In Numbers 16, Korah and a number of other men

rose up before Moses and rebelled against the Lord. In Verse 30, we read of the results:

> "But if the Lord creates something new, and the ground opens its mouth and swallows them up with all that belongs to them, and they go down alive into Sheol, then you shall know that these men have despised the Lord."

And that's exactly what happened. They were swallowed up in the ground, and the fact is this was no normal earthquake. The Word says the ground closed up after them as if they never were.

They got what they deserved.

In Revelation 11, a great calamity is predicted to come upon the enemies of the Lord. In Verse 13 we read:

> "And at that hour there was a great earthquake, and a tenth of the city fell. Seven thousand people were killed in the earthquake, and the rest were terrified and gave glory to the God of heaven."

It took the fist of the Lord taking seven thousand people in the earthquake before the rest gave glory to the God of heaven.

They got what was coming to them.

In Acts 16, Paul and Silas find themselves in prison. They are singing hymns to God and praying in loud voices. Verse 26 tells us:

> ". . . and suddenly there was a great earthquake, so that the foundations of the prison were shaken. And immediately all the doors were opened, and everyone's bonds were unfastened."

Even in their calamity, Paul and Silas put God first, and his earthquake released them from their prison bonds.

That got what they deserved.

In Matthew 28, Jesus has been crucified, and he is buried in a tomb. Verse 2 tells us:

> "And behold, there was a great earthquake, for an angel of the Lord descended from heaven and came and rolled back the stone and sat on it."

Guess what he allowed to come out? It was Jesus, the Son of God, resurrected from the dead, and returned to bring us the salvation of the cross and eternal life in his name forevermore!

God gave us exactly what was coming to us.

If we come to Jesus and repent of our sins, we get

what we deserve. We get Jesus. It's all part of God's generous payout plan.

In summary, the earthquake is unimportant. It's what we get out of it that makes us shine for Jesus.

Light Bulb Moment

Our spiritual high yield accounts are those that are invested in the work of Christ on this earth.

High Yield Accounts

When investing for the future, there are several ways we can go. We can stuff our money in our mattress, and when we go to sleep at night, we will know right where it is. However, that money will be worth exactly the same twenty years from now as it is today.

We will do better to invest it in a high yield account that will accrue interest and dividends, so that when we need to draw against our funds, we have far more available than we need.

The Bible addresses our spiritual investment options in several ways. Of course, the most obvious thing we can do is accept Christ as our savior and gain heaven as our reward. Still, there are other things the Word speaks to, also.

High Yield Account Opportunity #1:

> James 1:27 gives us a clear prospectus on what we can do to make our spiritual investments work as hard for us as possible. He tells us that for religion to be pure and undefiled before God, there are three things we must do. 1. We must visit orphans. 2. We must keep watch over widows. 3. We must keep ourselves unstained from the world.

High Yield Account Opportunity #2:

> 2 Timothy 3:16 spells out our investment opportunity, telling us the best accounts and how to access them. We must trust that all Scripture is breathed out by God, and that we can use every word to teach others about him, to offer reproof when others slip up, for correction of erroneous investment strategies, and to train the inexperienced to walk in the footsteps of Jesus.

High Yield Account Opportunity #3:

> Proverbs 1:1-7 tells us where our best investment advice comes from, for all wisdom, all wise dealing, all prudence, and all increase in learning comes from the fear of the Lord, for in that fear is where all knowledge begins.

There is no better future investment than in our spiritual relationship with God. We can increase our yield by remembering these three simple truths: Remain undefiled before God; look to the Scripture for understanding; and retain a healthy fear of the Lord.

What is our healthy fear of the Lord? Is it a quivering, hide under the table, sweaty armpits sort of fear? Absolutely not. The fear of the Lord is the awareness that he will hold our feet to the fire for the knowledge he has blessed us with. When we get a grasp on that, we will find our motivation to keep his truths held high before all men.

In summary, our spiritual high yield accounts are those that are invested in the work of Christ on this earth. We will cash them in when we reach the Gates of Glory.

Light Bulb Moment

We must respect the integrity of the written word of God, because the manuscript is the legal property of the greatest being in the universe.

Infringing God's Copyright

When an author pens a manuscript, he or she owns the rights to the words in that manuscript. No one else can use, rewrite, or summarize the material without the author's specific permission. No one can remove parts they do not like, and in the same manner, no one can add words to enhance what's already there.

One interesting aspect of copyright law is that the author does not have to be the person who actually pens the manuscript. If Company A pays an employee to write a story, then Company A is the legal author of the story, and the employee has no rights at all to the manuscript.

Who is the author of the Bible? We understand without question that the hands of Moses, David, Paul, and John wrote the words we revere today. Those men and a hundred others penned the manuscript, but the copyright is God's. The rights to the Bible belong to him, and we cannot change them because we do not like what they say, or we feel they are incomplete.

Here are four proofs that we must not infringe God's copyright:

Infringement Proof #1:

> 2 Timothy 3:16 tells us that "all Scripture is breathed out by God and profitable for teaching, for reproof, for correction, and for training in righteousness."
>
> All means all. We cannot exclude a single verse.

Infringement Proof #2:

> Revelation 22:19 warns us that "if anyone takes away from the words of the book of this prophecy, God will take away his share in the tree of life and in the holy city, which are described in this book."
>
> God's words are his own, for he is the authority that is the legal owner of each and every word in the Bible.

Infringement Proof #3:

Proverbs 30:6 reminds us that the Scriptures are complete. "Do not add to his words, lest he rebuke you and you be found a liar."

The words penned two and more thousand years ago do not need to be updated for a modern world. Their lessons are still pertinent to us today.

Infringement Proof #4:

Hebrews 4:12 gives us the true power of God's written manuscript. "For the word of God is living and active, sharper than any two-edged sword, piercing to the division of soul and of spirit, of joints and of marrow, and discerning the thoughts and intentions of the heart."

God's Word already has the power to divide right from wrong and bring the unbeliever to Christ. We do not need to try to rewrite God's manuscript for him.

God is the author of the Bible. The men who penned the words worked for the almighty Father, and in their faith, they relinquished their author's rights to the one who paid them with salvation and life everlasting. We have no need to make any changes, because the Word says exactly what God means it to say.

In summary, we must respect the integrity of the written word of God, because the manuscript is the legal property of the greatest being in the universe.

Light Bulb Moment

God not only draws us to him; he repels that which tries to destroy us.

Magnetic Properties of God

Magnetism is an amazing phenomenon. Hold up a sliver of a magnet, and it always points due north. Energize it with superconductive techniques, and it will remain permanently suspended around an object, neither touching nor falling away.

Magnetism does more for our planet, though. It creates the Northern Lights. In Iceland, during the long winter darkness, the fantastic display is visible the entire season.

Wow! And here is something even better: The amazing thing is not that magnets behave as they do. The truly amazing, astounding reality is that those very behaviors are also found in our incredible God.

Let's look to the scriptures for evidence of God's magnetic properties:

Magnetic Example #1:

Everything about our existence points to God. John 3:16 says, "For God so loved the world, that he gave his only Son, that whoever believes in him should not perish but have eternal life."

Jesus is the only goal worth striving for. He pulls us his direction. We can fight his drawing power, and we can skew off in our own direction, but he always continues to draw us toward him.

Magnetic Example #2:

John 10:30 says: "I and the Father are one." They are magnets, superconductively suspended in tandem, unable to be broken apart.

Colossians 1:15-17 continues with, "He is the image of the invisible God, the firstborn of all creation. For by him all things were created, in heaven and on earth, visible and invisible, whether thrones or dominions or rulers or authorities—all things were created through him and for him. And he is before all things, and in him all things hold together."

There is no distinction between Jesus and his Father. If we have seen one, we have seen the other. They act in accord with each other's wishes. We can depend on both to be in agreement on everything and at all times.

Magnetic Example #3:

> God shines with the beauty of his glory, at no time more spectacularly than when we are in the middle of the darkest times of our lives. In fact, just as the residents of Iceland cannot see the Northern Lights in the warmth of summer, we find the real power of God in our troubled hours.
>
> Revelation 21:2 gives us an apt description: "And I saw the holy city, new Jerusalem, coming down out of heaven from God, prepared as a bride adorned for her husband."
>
> A few verses later, Revelation 21:11 compares his beauty to something that can only be the Northern Lights of heaven: "Having the glory of God, its radiance like a most rare jewel, like a jasper, clear as crystal."

We can play tricks with magnetism, make electricity with magnetism, and launch airplanes off aircraft carriers with magnetism. All that is fantastic, but the most important thing magnetism does for us is protect Earth from deadly bombardments of solar radiation. Again, that's God, for he is the one that protects us from the deadly bombardments of the devil.

And amazingly, that's when he shows up most brilliantly in all his glorious colors.

In summary, God not only draws us to him; he repels that which tries to destroy us.

Light Bulb Moment

We need to continue to bow in supplication, so that every person has the opportunity to know Jesus as his Savior and King.

One More Time, Mommy

Any mother can relate to these words: "One more time, Mommy." Whether they come while visiting the swing set at the park, or after a favorite bedtime story, they mean the same thing. It's too soon for the fun to end.

We are all like that. We want to keep the good times rolling. That's why we eat one more slice of pizza, catch the double feature, or buy a specialty car that's no more than an expensive toy. We've had fun at something we've enjoyed, and we don't want the thrill to end.

Do we ever cry, "One more time," to God? Have we had a spiritual experience we enjoyed so much we didn't want it to end?

Let's see if we can reawaken some of those feelings, by reminding ourselves of the special times we've spent with God. Let's look for that memory when we enjoyed God's presence so much that we didn't want it to end.

Romans 6:23 is a good place to start.

> "For the wages of sin is death, but the free gift of God is eternal life in Christ Jesus our Lord."

> We all love something when it's free, and God gives us the best freebie of all. He offers us eternal life.

John 3:16 tells us his plan.

> "For God so loved the world, that he gave his only Son, that whoever believes in him should not perish but have eternal life."

> When we profess our faith, we are changed. We are welcomed into life, and death is forever cast aside.

Romans 5:8 illustrates the degree of God's love for us.

> "But God shows his love for us in that while we were still sinners, Christ died for us."

> We don't have to prove ourselves to God. He loves us unconditionally. All we have to do is

love him back.

Acts 2:38 opens the door to our workout room.

> "And Peter said to them, 'Repent and be baptized every one of you in the name of Jesus Christ for the forgiveness of your sins, and you will receive the gift of the Holy Spirit.' "

> We can be pumped-up Christians, well-muscled and full of vigor in him. Better yet, the Holy Spirit will build our strength for us.

2 Timothy 2:15 reveals how simple it is to meet God's standards.

> "Do your best to present yourself to God as one approved, a worker who has no need to be ashamed, rightly handling the word of truth."

> When we share the truth of God's message, and we live a clean life, we will receive God's stamp of approval.

John 3:3 answers the argument that we do not need to follow Christ.

> "Jesus answered him, 'Truly, truly, I say to you, unless one is born again he cannot see the kingdom of God.' "

We have only one way to heaven, and it comes through the cross and Jesus. Any other way is a lie, and it will lead us to destruction.

1 John 1:8 peels back our self-righteousness, so that we may see ourselves as we are.

> "If we say we have no sin, we deceive ourselves, and the truth is not in us."

A mirror is our best tool, and the best mirror is the Word of God. If we study the Bible, we can compare ourselves to the saints of God and know how we stand in God's eyes.

2 Peter 3:9 assures us that God will fulfill every guarantee in his Word.

> "The Lord is not slow to fulfill his promise as some count slowness, but is patient toward you, not wishing that any should perish, but that all should reach repentance."

We do not look forward to an empty death, as some say. Instead, we look forward to a new life of eternity spent with the Father. Everyone is welcome to come along.

2 Timothy 3:16-17 points out our handbook, so that we can understand every step of the directions.

"All Scripture is breathed out by God and profitable for teaching, for reproof, for correction, and for training in righteousness, that the man of God may be competent, equipped for every good work."

The world's religious confusion is from the devil, for he wishes to divide us. What is important is the truth in the Word, and that is simple. We must show the love of Christ to everyone we meet.

Ephesians 2:8-9 lays out the simplicity of our salvation.

"For by grace you have been saved through faith. And this is not your own doing; it is the gift of God, not a result of works, so that no one may boast."

Our success in Christ has nothing to do with us. Rather, it has everything to do with God. When we have faith, we have everything God needs to transform us to be like him.

Let's keep the spiritual good times rolling. Let's look back at the fun we've had with God, and let's tell him, "One more time, please."

In summary, we need to continue to bow in

supplication, so that every person has the opportunity to know Jesus as his Savior and King.

Light Bulb Moment

When we wear the colors of Jesus, we will make a difference in the world.

Our Fine Feathered Friends

To begin the message, we can tell the difference between winter, summer, spring, and fall, and we don't even have to open our eyes.

We only need to listen with our ears.

It's birdsong—or the lack of it—that tells us that winter is here. Or, conversely, it tells us that spring has arrived. The lilting songs of the nightingale and the mockingbird drifting through our screens throughout the summer are a pleasant reminder of the season. In the fall? The recurring melodies are a reminder that the season is soon to change.

In winter, we wait for the first trill of that first bird to know the long cold is about to release its grip on the earth.

Yet what other fine feathered friends do we have that help us through the seasons of life?

Psalm 91:11 tells us:

> "For he will command his angels concerning you to guard you in all your ways."

Angels! They are the precursors to the changes we face in life. They come and they go, and if we pay attention to their movements, we can sense the upcoming seasons of our lives.

Hebrews 13:2 reminds us:

> "Do not neglect to show hospitality to strangers, for thereby some have entertained angels unawares."

God sends his messengers to us on an "as needed" basis. They will be there in the most unexpected situations. It may not be in a time of need. Rather, it may be in a season of excess. How will we treat his delegates, then? That is a test of our true character.

Acts 8:26 shows us an angel in action:

> "Now an angel of the Lord said to Philip, 'Rise and go toward the south to the road that goes down from Jerusalem to Gaza.' "

God's angels will nudge us into our new seasons. If we listen to their songs, we will find ourselves walking the paths God has for us.

Matthew 24:31 assures us we will not miss his new season:

> "And he will send out his angels with a loud trumpet call, and they will gather his elect from the four winds, from one end of heaven to the other."

God speaks to us with a still, small voice, but the seasons of our lives come upon us with the sounds of a crashing cymbal. We cannot miss what God has in store for us.

The Word is filled with mention of the exploits of God's angels. However, these final two examples are both found in 2 Kings and bring home just how important it is to trust in the angels of the Lord. God's messengers are not just delivery boys and soft-skinned puffs of light to hover over our children's beds at night. No, they are much, much more.

2 Kings 6:17 reveals to us what we cannot see:

> "Then Elisha prayed and said, 'O Lord, please open his eyes that he may see.' So the Lord opened the eyes of the young man, and he saw, and behold, the mountain was full of horses and

chariots of fire all around Elisha."

Those horses and chariots of fire? They were the angels of the Lord. Elisha beheld them, and he knew the power of their strong arms. Nothing could successfully war against the glittering swords of the holy ones.

2 Kings 19:35 demonstrates how powerful just one of God's angels can be:

"And that night the angel of the Lord went out and struck down 185,000 in the camp of the Assyrians. And when people arose early in the morning, behold, these were all dead bodies."

God didn't need to send an army of angels to defeat the hoard of Assyrians. No, all he needed was one of his messengers, and the enemy was wiped from the scene, bringing a season of victory to the children of Israel.

That brings us back to Psalm 91:11. We don't have only one angel standing guard over us. God's Word says:

"For he will command his *angels* concerning you to guard you in all your ways."

If one angel can take out 185,000 Assyrians, we are

given the assurance we have nothing to fear. We have all of God's army watching over us.

In summary, when God's angels are with us, we have no better friends to stand at our side.

Light Bulb Moment

When Jesus says this is not our home, he's telling it the way it is. We're strangers in a strange land, and that's exactly the way we want it to be.

Stranger in a Strange Land

Visit Roswell, New Mexico, and just try to get away without an alien artifact for a souvenir. Turn on the television, anytime, anywhere, and there are shows that claim to track the landings of UFOs all over the planet.

Why, these shows even tell us that it was with the help of UFO spaceships that the pyramids were constructed. No way could humanity have completed such an awesome task. Men 4,000 years ago simply didn't have the skills.

Those of us with saner thoughts laugh, some openly, and others behind our smiles, but we do laugh. Who do these fools think will believe them? UFOs? Really? Get a grip, man. This is the 21st century! We know better.

But are we right? Dare we ask that question? Is it

possible ... just possible that ancient aliens might have indeed visited planet earth?

Let's see what the Word of God says:

Genesis 1:1. "In the beginning, God created the heavens and the earth."

Now, hold on a minute, we say. That's God, not an alien.

But wait! What is an alien if not a creature from another world, one not human and most certainly different than you and me? So, let's see what else the Word says.

Genesis 2:7. "Then the Lord God formed the man of dust from the ground and breathed into his nostrils the breath of life, and the man became a living creature."

How does this tie in? In all the reports of UFOs, it seems the aliens always have some sort of unusual power, something that humanity can't do. ESP or telekinesis. Well, how about making dust walk and talk? That's pretty alien, by anyone's measure.

There's more, though. Check out this verse:

Revelation 5:6. "I saw a Lamb standing, as though it had been slain, with seven horns and with seven eyes."

A seven-eyed creature with seven horns. Bet no one on earth has ever seen one of those. What's this verse describing? God, of course, a being that is so alien we cannot even recognize his shape or form.

If all that hasn't convinced you, this last doozy will do the trick.

Acts 2:2-4. "Suddenly there came from heaven a sound like a mighty rushing wind . . . and they were all filled with the Holy Spirit . . ."

Holy ghost busters shazzaam! Something invisible invades the believers to live inside them! It's goose bumps time!

Are we seeing the whole picture, yet? This is God we're talking about. He's way more than human. That's why he says this isn't our home. When we come to him, we become like him, and that makes us strangers in a strange land.

Let's work our goose bumps down and jump for joy. When he comes back at the end of days, we'll be riding his blazing UFO into the sky. Don't believe that? Read it in 2 Kings 2:11. "Chariots of fire and horses of fire separated the two of them. And Elijah went up by a whirlwind into heaven."

The goose bumps should be popping out now, with no hope of getting them under control!

In summary, when Jesus says this is not our home, he's telling it the way it is. We're strangers in a strange land, and that's exactly the way we want it to be.

Light Bulb Moment

Sin is a snake that will encumber us. We must cast it aside to find freedom in Christ.

The Arms of the Snake

In June of 2014, two cars went up for sale on a televised automobile auction. They were both from the same collector, and both had been bought and still belonged to the original owner. One was a 45-year-old GTO and the other a 25-year-old Porsche.

Both cars were immaculate. The GTO had been given professional modifications to make it competitive with any new car on the road today. The Porsche had less than 20,000 miles on it and was considered the best example of a comparable model year Porsche in existence.

Yet, this collector was willing to let these iconic cars go to the highest bidder. Why?

He and his wife had become entwined in the arms of the snake. Their possessions had begun to own them. Their grandchildren lived in a distant state, and they were forced to make a decision: the snake of earthly possessions or the family they loved.

They decided to cast off the snake and reach for what was truly important in this life, the arms of those that loved them. Only then could they be free to pursue the things they truly valued. As long as they held onto those valuable cars, their actions would be dictated by them, and they would not be free.

Sin does that to us in the exact same way. It's a snake that wraps us in its arms, and it will not let us go. We lose our freedom, and we can only regain it when we cast aside that which keeps us bound.

The Word gives us fair warning with regards to one sin, that of intoxication. Read along in the following three verses:

Wine Warning #1:

> Proverbs 20:1. "Wine is a mocker, strong drink a brawler, and whoever is led astray by it is not wise."

Wine Warning #2:

> Isaiah 5:11. "Woe to those who rise early in the morning, that they may run after strong drink,

who tarry late into the evening as wine inflames them!"

Wine Warning #3:

Galatians 5:21. "Envy, drunkenness, orgies, and things like these. I warn you, as I warned you before, that those who do such things will not inherit the kingdom of God."

However, there is an alternative given to us, one that we can rejoice in.

Ephesians 5:18. "And do not get drunk with wine, for that is debauchery, but be filled with the Spirit."

The cars that couple put in the automobile auction were not evil. However, what they owned had begun to own them. When we let the things of this world control who we are and what we do for God, then it's time to auction them off and let God be our rock and solid foundation, for only in him can we find the freedom to become who he wants us to be.

In summary, sin is a snake that will encumber us. We must cast it aside to find freedom in Christ.

Light Bulb Moment

Who needs the corner office? We've got Jesus, and that's better by far.

The Big Cheese

Being the boss is nice. We get the best parking spot, can afford the best car, and that corner office? It comes with the job.

We like being the big cheese.

Even in our homes, being the big cheese means our word is law, and we get to control the purse strings, the television remote, and the thermostat. We're the one who gets final say in our vacation plans.

What about in the church? How does being the big cheese work there? There are five references from Revelation that are relevant here.

Relevant Reference #1:

> Revelation 21:9. "Then came one of the seven angels who had the seven bowls full of the seven last plagues and spoke to me, saying, 'Come, I

will show you the Bride, the wife of the Lamb.'"

We need to pay attention to the numbers. The angel is one of seven. The Bride is the big cheese.

Relevant Reference #2:

Revelation 21:3. "And I heard a loud voice from the throne saying, 'Behold, the dwelling place of God is with man. He will dwell with them, and they will be his people, and God himself will be with them as their God.'"

Again, it's about the numbers. God will be the one and only god. He gets the best parking space.

Relevant Reference #3:

Revelation 5:6. "And between the throne and the four living creatures and among the elders I saw a Lamb standing, as though it had been slain, with seven horns and with seven eyes, which are the seven spirits of God sent out into all the earth."

How many lambs did we note here? Ah, it's the big cheese. The seven spirits are secondary. The remote is not theirs to control.

Relevant Reference #4:

> Revelation 3:1. "And to the angel of the church in Sardis write: 'The words of him who has the seven spirits of God and the seven stars. I know your works. You have the reputation of being alive, but you are dead.' "

> In this passage, the big cheese has his hand on the thermostat, and the temperature is about to go up. Everyone else had better pay attention.

Relevant Reference #5:

> Revelation 2:1-2. "To the angel of the church in Ephesus write: 'The words of him who holds the seven stars in his right hand, who walks among the seven golden lampstands. I know your works, your toil and your patient endurance, and how you cannot bear with those who are evil, but have tested those who call themselves apostles and are not, and found them to be false.' "

> We toil as a unit; not in a singular fashion, but as a team. We are not the big cheese; rather, we are the tiny cheese squares. Only in unity can we find success in any measure.

Let's step away from Revelation for a moment and

look at the spoken words of Jesus. He sums it up quite well in Matthew 23:8.

> "But you are not to be called rabbi, for you have one teacher, and you are all brothers."

Once more, it's about the numbers. Singular rabbi. Plural brothers. By Jesus' own words, there is one big cheese, but there are lots of little cheese-lets. He's the big cheese. We are the Velveeta squares.

Let's let God remain in control. It's the job he's best at, one that we couldn't do if we tried.

In summary, who needs the corner office? We've got Jesus, and that's better by far.

Light Bulb Moment

When Jesus battles at our side, he stacks the deck in our favor, and we always win.

The Devil's Black Eye

To begin the message, our spiritual existence is a battlefield. Shells explode around us, and we can hardly raise our heads out of our foxholes. When we put on our armor, it weighs so heavily on our shoulders that we are exhausted before the day even gets started.

Other times, we feel we are going high-speed, bent for a horrific crash, if we can't get off the racetrack. Our hands are on the wheel, but we're no longer sure if we're in control, and we don't dare slow down. We know what's behind us, and it's frightening.

Or we're on the field, and half-time is over. The whistle blows, and we discover we've got the ball in our hands. We look up to see every player on the opposing team growling at us, and we know for certain we're going to wind up at the bottom of the pile.

What we have to understand is that God has placed us in a boxing ring, and he's put iron plate in our gloves. When we pull our hand back to swing, it will be heavy, and we will have to put extra muscle in our thrust. However, when it hits the devil's face, he will go down like a log, and he will be out like a light.

Matthew 10:28 cautions us to "fear him who can destroy both soul and body in hell." But note this: Nowhere are we told to run from him. Search out the words of Jesus, and you will not find any location that says to put our tails between our legs and whimper in defeat.

Rather, read in James 4:7, where it tells us to resist the devil, and he will flee from us.

That should get our blood flowing. Shells can explode all around us, but the armor of the Lord suddenly becomes as lightweight as a feather. Our protection no longer weighs us down.

On that racetrack, God supercharges our engine, and we don't have to worry about who's behind us, because they can't catch up, anyway.

That football game? We're already to the goal line,

and we can slam that ball to the ground. The touchdown is already ours.

And what about that boxing glove? Are we cheating? No! God is ensuring that we will rise in glorious victory. When the devil falls before us with his eyes blackened and his nose bleeding, we won't notice. We'll be held high on the shoulders of the saints, and the crowd will be cheering for us.

The victory will be ours, and Jesus will be the reason!

In summary, when Jesus battles at our side, he stacks the deck in our favor, and we always win.

Light Bulb Moment

When we wear the colors of Jesus, we will make a difference in the world.

The Man in Purple

What does it matter the color we paint our houses? Or the cars we drive?

Red, blue, or orange, it's just a color.

Yet, in some neighborhoods, to wear certain colors means we identify with a criminal gang. Sport the wrong colors, and we can spark a conflagration of events, one we never intended.

Do we drive a red automobile? Pay attention to the rules of the road, then, for studies show that red cars attract officers' attention. That's the one color that receives more citations than all other colors.

What about purple? What should purple signify to us?

Let's start with this distressing image in John 19:2:

> "And the soldiers twisted together a crown of

thorns and put it on his head and arrayed him in a purple robe."

Who wants to wear purple? Especially if our accessory must be a twisted crown of thorns?

However, let's also look at four passages from the Book of Revelations:

> "The one who conquers, I will grant him to sit with me on my throne, as I also conquered and sat down with my Father on his throne." Revelation 3:21.

> "And when he had taken the scroll, the four living creatures and the twenty-four elders fell down before the Lamb, each holding a harp, and golden bowls full of incense, which are the prayers of the saints." Revelation 5:8.

> "And the great dragon was thrown down, that ancient serpent, who is called the devil and Satan, the deceiver of the whole world—he was thrown down to the earth, and his angels were thrown down with him." Revelation 12:9.

> "And he seized the dragon, that ancient serpent, who is the devil and Satan, and bound him for a thousand years." Revelation 20:2.

Now, where did that crown of thorns go? These

verses are all about the power of the Man in Purple. Pilate was making fun when he paraded Jesus before the people, but little did he know the import of his words in John 19:5:

> "So Jesus came out, wearing the crown of thorns and the purple robe. Pilate said to them, 'Behold the man!'"

Behold the man! By all means, behold the man, for he is the Son of God, the Mighty Redeemer, the Risen Christ, and the Glorious King of Kings.

Who wouldn't want to wear purple?

An elderly woman once ran with a group of peers whose unifying item of clothing was a purple hat. Their hats signified that they were not going quietly into the night, fading away into old people who had given up on life. Rather, they intended to be bold and brash, to make their mark on the world around them, and to make sure they were noticed.

That's what the color purple should mean to Christians. Jesus didn't choose his purple robe, but it said more about him than Pilate ever intended. Jesus did not go quietly into the night. His life was not ended upon the cross. Instead, he rose with majesty to make his mark on the world.

The best thing of all? Everyone noticed. Purple matters. Let's claim it for Christ.

In summary, when we wear the colors of Jesus, we will make a difference in the world.

Light Bulb Moment

When we truly understand what Jesus needs us to be to our fellow man, we will shine with his love, and we will draw them to the cross.

The Twelfth Stone

Twelve is a number of high standing in the world today. Twelve is the amount of eggs in a carton. Twelve inches are in a foot. Even the face of a clock has twelve numbers, ones repeated two times in each day.

The actual word twelve comes from the Germanic compound "twalif" meaning having two left over after sorting out ten. A group of twelve things is called a duodecad. In adjective form, we say duodecuple.

Those terms may be esoteric to most of us, but we understand the use of the term twelve quite well. We order our eggs, quote the length of objects, and even bake cupcakes in twelves. Need a larger quantity? Twelve dozen are known as a gross. We even have a term for twelve plus one: a baker's dozen.

Let's tie twelve into the Bible. Jacob had twelve sons, making up the twelve tribes of Israel. Jesus had twelve disciples. Even in the secular world, people recognize the twelve days of Christmas.

Where are the spiritual ramifications, though? How does the number twelve affect our walk with Christ?

Revelation 21:19-27 speaks of the New Jerusalem. In this passage, we read of twelve gates where stand twelve angels. The walls of the city have twelve foundations portraying the twelve names of the twelve apostles of the Lamb.

Then note the size of the city: 12,000 stadia. Its walls are 144 cubits (the total of twelve multiplied by twelve) and each of the twelve gates are made of twelve individual pearls.

Yet, within the foundation itself is the twelve we wish to look at today. The foundations of the city are adorned with twelve types of jewels. The first eleven are of wondrous beauty and exquisite form, but the twelfth is the most precious of them all.

Verse 20 in this passage tells us, "the fifth onyx, the sixth carnelian, the seventh chrysolite, the eighth beryl, the ninth topaz, the tenth chrysoprase, the eleventh jacinth, the twelfth amethyst."

This is a partial listing of the stones in the foundations. Amethyst is listed as the final one, coming in the twelfth and final position. Is there any way this is accidental? Of course not.

Let's look at a passage from a previous MyChurchNotes.net article titled, "God's Gemstones." This article breaks down the religious significance of each of the stones in the foundations of the coming masterpiece of New Jerusalem. Let's reread what it says about amethyst:

> "Iron and aluminum give the amethyst its brilliant purple color. The more iron we find in the mineral, the more purple it shines."

How magnificent is that? Iron, one of the hardest and most versatile substances we know, one that makes up the backbone of our modern day industrial infrastructure, and aluminum, one of the softest and most malleable metals in existence, combine to make us shine brilliantly for Christ. We have to be both iron and aluminum in order to be what God wants us to be. When the devil comes at us with his wiles and tries to sideline us, we must have spiritual backbones of iron. Yet, when our fellow humans stumble against us, we must be soft enough that we can mold the message of Christ to their needs, so that we do not drive them from the cross with our religious intolerance and inflexibility.

Iron and aluminum. That's what good Christians are made of. We are the brightly shining amethyst that makes up the final and most beautiful of the stones in the foundation of the greatest of the cities ever built or ever to come.

Let's make sure our neighbors and coworkers can see us shine with the beauty of Jesus each and every day.

In summary, when we truly understand what Jesus needs us to be to our fellow man, we will shine with his love, and we will draw them to the cross.

Light Bulb Moment

When we fill up with Jesus and the world squeezes us, the Son of God will burst forth every time.

Volcanic Christianity

Volcanoes are amazing, and it's not why we think.

Yes, we see the plumes of smoke, and on the news reports, we read of homes consumed by oozing rivers of lava. Volcanoes are dangerous, and to live next to one? Not me, not ever, and not on your life.

Yet, to live near a volcano is to gain a toehold on the choice qualities of life. Volcanic ash makes the soil nearby some of the most productive in the world. And beauty? There is no greater beauty that we can find. Imagine Hawaii or Fiji or the great volcanic mountains of the Northwest along the coast of the United States and Canada.

Yet, while Fiji might be perfectly safe, Hawaii has the world's most active volcano, one that regularly eats homes built in its path. Google Mount St. Helens, and half of it was blown away in the latter part of the 20th century. It's a volcano, always ready to erupt once again.

Who can forget the tales of Pompeii? The final moments of that ancient city have become an indelible moment in the history of our world. Thousands of years have passed, and we can still identify with the terror and the pain of being buried alive in burning ash and molten stone.

Even all that's not what makes volcanoes so amazing. When an eruption happens, we get to experience something that occurs at no other time on the face of our planet. The earth slings out a little bit of its core. We get to see what our world is really like on the inside.

What comes out of a volcano is what our magnificent world is really made of. It's the truth that all the forests and reefs and snow-covered slopes can't disguise. We see the reality show of life, one that reveals the inner workings of God's creation in a way that he can show us like no one else can.

It's terrifying, incredible, and beautiful all at the same time. In a word, it's amazing.

What does the world see when our volcano erupts? Yes, we all have one. Some of us have several. A few of us are encircled by them. Our emotions, our families, everything we touch as we go through life. All are potential volcanoes, ready to show the world just who we are inside.

We are even born from a volcano. Read in Genesis 3:16:

> "To the woman he said, 'I will surely multiply your pain in childbearing; in pain you shall bring forth children. Your desire shall be for your husband, and he shall rule over you.' "

If childbirth is not a volcano, then for millennia, women have cried out in vain, for no other reason than to entertain the world. Let's ask, what does the world see in that eruption? What is the reality we have brought forth? How do we train up our children? They reflect who we are. Just ask any teacher who sits through a parent-teacher conference. The child is a mirror of the parent, in more ways than many parents want to own.

We are also born from God's volcano. Read in Genesis 2:7:

> "Then the Lord God formed the man of dust from the ground and breathed into his nostrils the breath of life, and the man became a living creature."

We reflect God as surely as our children reflect us.

His nature is our nature. What we feel, he feels. What we desire, he desires. However, just as a child can choose to alienate herself from her parents, so we can alienate ourselves from God. We can chase our own desires, even while at our core, we remain a singular creation that reflects the source of humanity's creation.

That's why God continually calls us back to him. Read in 1 John 1:9:

> "If we confess our sins, he is faithful and just to forgive us our sins and to cleanse us from all unrighteousness."

Take a rock. Any rock. Paint it, plate it with gold, throw it in a cesspool. It becomes covered with what touches it. We see it as disgusting, and we toss it aside. Yet, scour it with the sands of the desert, scorch it with the heat of the sun, or shower it beneath pounding waterfalls, and we will get the original rock back. Remove the gunk, and it's no longer junk.

It becomes something we can treasure once more.

At those times in life when volcanic eruptions show the world just who we are inside, let's endeavor to make sure we show Jesus. When we're made of him, that's what will come out every time.

In summary, when we fill up with Jesus and the world squeezes us, the Son of God will burst forth every time.

Coming to Christ
In Three Easy Steps

If you do not know Christ as your personal savior, there is no better time than the present to turn your life over to him.

- Step 1 is to admit that you are human, God is God, and you need his grace.
- Step 2 is to place your belief in him. You must accept that he is the Son of the Eternal God, and through his death on the cross, he can give you new life.
- Step 3 is to turn from your previous ways and receive the hope of Jesus' power in you.

Fill in the following information as a testament to your decision to accept Jesus as your Savior.

I, _____, accept Jesus
              print your full name

as my personal savior on _____.
                                today's date

_____
             your signature

Look for these additional topics on the MyChurchNotes.net website:

2 Timothy
Beatitudes
Discipleship
Evangelism
Faith
Family
Healing
Hope
Kingdom of God
Money
Prayer
Relationships
Repentance
Salvation
Worship

MyChurchNotes.net is a faith-based ministry founded on a belief in the Father, the Son, and the Holy Spirit. All MyChurchNotes.net articles are based on Scripture and created especially for MyChurchNotes.net.

Our Mission Statement is to take the Word of God into all the nations, and proclaim that he is Lord!

If you enjoyed
God Offers His Kingdom to All,
please visit us at our website:

www.MyChurchNotes.net

We look forward to hearing from you.

Website and Publication Powered by:

Freedom in Imagination, Planning, and Execution · Never One of the Crowd

Bright Herd . . . for All Your Website and Media Design Needs.
www.brightherd.com
contact@brightherd.com

www.ingramcontent.com/pod-product-compliance
Lightning Source LLC
Chambersburg PA
CBHW061445040426
42450CB00007B/1228